Contents

Introduction

Cardiovascular disease can result from chronic renal disease, kidney failure, inflammation, etc. It is the primary cause of death and irreversible damage caused to some chronic uremic patients. The mortality rate is often about sixty-five times greater in people between 45–54 years old and five hundred times higher in younger people!

Kidney diseases and complications affect as much as 10% of the population in the world today. The kidneys, which are small compared to some other body organs, are involved in some heavy-duty work to regulate certain bodily products in the body. This means that individuals with compromised kidneys should do everything in their power to aid this already tedious function.

For medical patients with chronic renal failure or simply failed kidneys, some dietary requirements have to be followed to suppress the damage exerted by the cardiovascular risk factors and prevent the complete breakdown of the excretory system. Such individuals are encouraged to cut down on the amount of waste in their blood as much as possible. When this precaution is not taken, the kidneys will fail to work properly, and when this happens, waste starts to build up in the body leading to a lot of complications and even death in critical situations.

A high build-up of wastes will adversely affect a patient's electrolyte level. This necessity to reduce metabolic wastes facilitates the need for a unique diet for high-risk patients with renal failure and cardiovascular damage. This diet is called the renal diet, kidney diet, or dialysis diet.

The dietary restrictions emphasized by the renal diet involves restrictions on sodium, protein, and phosphorus. At the same time, a renal diet could emphasize the consumption of high-quality proteins.

The restrictions in kidney diets are also said to encourage the build-up of biological properties that are anti-inflammatory and antioxidant, which may be helpful in slowing down the progress of the renal disease. A low protein diet may just be the difference between life and death for someone with renal failure and/or kidney problems.

What is the Renal Diet About?

The renal diet is a diet formulated from a combination of medical techniques and maneuvers aimed towards treating the dangers of cardiovascular risk. The strategies used in the formulation of these diets are either scientific or non-scientific, but with the main aim of stopping the cardiovascular system's breakdown.

The renal diet plays a vital role in protecting the full capacity and capability of the remaining functions still operative in the damaged cardiovascular system of a weak patient. Most times, they are even in need of dialysis.

The renal diet not only entails restricting the protein intake of a patient, but it also involves a nutritional system that looks tricky at first but gets simpler once followed regularly and completely. Apart from the reduction of protein and protein-rich supplements, the use of sodium and phosphorus will also have to be cut down while the consumption of plant-based food materials has to be increased.

The kidney diet is a meal that is low in sodium, protein, and phosphorus but with the necessary vitamins, amino acid supplements, and keto acids for balanced nutrition. Calcium carbonate and iron are also added to this meal to give renal failure patients the strength needed to recover completely with treatment.

Each diet has certain variations, depending on the severity of the ailment in the patient and also the level and history of kidney damage. However, the crux of the situation is the adoption of a renal diet that is kidney-friendly enough to result in the reduction of waste products infused into the blood.

The renal diet boosts the available functions of the kidney while simultaneously preventing the risk of more damage. And although there might be different variations of the dietary restrictions, the primary nutrients that need to be reduced for this diet's success are sodium, protein, potassium, and phosphorus.

Benefits of the Renal Diet

The renal diet has a bunch of positive effects on patients that are concerned with cardiovascular risk factors. Let us look at some of these effects in detail:

- **The Renal Diet Reduces the Risk of Hypertension in Patients.**

Patients with cardiovascular risk factors often fall prey to hypertension's torment, especially when treatment has not yet begun for their ailment. Apart from the enormous damages already caused by the cardiovascular damages/failures, hypertension can also cause a few more harms like microalbuminuria, increased oxidative stress, left ventricular hypertrophy, etc., all contributing to the eventual advancement of renal damage.

With the sodium restrictions imposed by the renal diet, there is a greater chance for patients with renal failure or other cardiovascular issues to respond to anti-hypertensive treatment. The nature of the diet also contributes to the reduction of blood pressure levels in these patients. These reductions in blood pressure levels occur in both patients that are either healthy or hypertensive.

- **The Renal Diet Slows Down the Progress of Diabetes and Corrects Insulin Resistance**

One of the events that occur when a patient is experiencing cardiovascular failure/complications is the body's resistance to insulin treatment. This is one of the most potent symptoms of renal disease. The renal diet serves to progress treatment for diabetic patients because it is known to reduce hyperglycemia and correct the system's insulin resistance due to the increased sensitivity to insulin.

To prevent the deformity associated with further failure in these body systems, the lowering of insulin sensitivity and the increase of energy production in cardiovascular disease patients have to be observed.

- **Renal Diet Reduces the Risk of Anemia**

Anemia is one of the connecting factors to the severity of medical cases involving cardiovascular problems. The medical experts have noted that when the risk of anemia is earlier checked using preventive/healing medicine, the danger of the disease progressing into the later stages is reduced. The renal diet combats low hemoglobin levels, which promote the onset of left ventricular growth. For positive effects, this diet is based on the decrease of phosphorus intake, and for strength, the increased intake of calcium salts.

Another thing that is thought to play an essential role in the successful control of anemia in renal failure patients is the low production of waste products due to the catabolism of healthy protein levels.

- **Calcium-Phosphate Irregularities are Corrected Using Renal Diet**

Hyperphosphatemia, which is the instability of calcium-phosphate metabolism, is an ailment that occurs in patients with chronic renal failure. What it entails is the escalation of the calcium-phosphate products and the increased PTH levels of the serum.

This ailment is very important in the discussion of risk factors associated with renal failure. For Hyperphosphatemia to be a problem in these patients' cases, the phosphate balance has to be on the positive side (this also causes calcium-phosphate tissue precipitation). Phosphate restrictions are better achieved by following the kidney diet.

- **The Renal Diet serves to Control Inflammation**

Most patients suffering from cardiovascular damage also run the risk of experiencing chronic inflammation of the body organs. These inflammations are often very severe, and if left unchecked, might even result in death.

To eat/ to Avoid

	To eat	To avoid
Milk products	Almond milk Rice milk Buttermilk (1/2 cup per day) Cottage cheese (1/4 cup per day) Cream cheese (2 oz. per day) Evaporated milk (1/4 cup per day) Light cream or half & half (1/2 cup per day) Milk (4 oz. per day) Yogurt (4 oz. per day)	Cheese Chocolate milk
Fruits (1/2 cup per serving)	Apple (1 small per serving) Pear Blackberries Blueberries Cherries Cranberries Grapes Lemons Peach Pineapple Plum (1 per serving) Strawberries Watermelon (1 cup per serving)	Apricots Bananas Coconut Dates Dried fruits Grapefruit Guava Figs Honeydew melon Kiwi Mango Nectarines Oranges Cantaloupe Prune

Bread, cereals	Sourdough bread	Brown rice
	White bread	Wild rice
	Italian, French bread	Bran cereals
	Cold cereal (no bran or high fiber) (3/4 cup per serving)	Cereals with nuts
	Cooked cereal (½ cup per serving)	Oatmeal
	Buckwheat	Dark rye bread
	Bulgur	Granola cereals/bars
	Couscous	High fiber crackers or bread
	Hamburger (1 per serving)	Pancakes
	Hot dog bun (1 per serving)	Waffles
	Popcorn, unsalted (1 ½ cup per serving)	Nut bread
	Crackers, unsalted	Salted crackers
	Tortillas (2 per serving)	Whole wheat bread
	White pasta (½ cup per serving)	Whole wheat cereals
	White rice (½ cup per serving)	Whole wheat pasta
		Instant noodles
		Frozen pizza

1 cup = 4 oz. 125 grms.

42 grams of protine per day.

Vegetables (½ cup per serving)	Asparagus (Limit to 3 times per week)	Artichoke
	Arugula	Avocado
	Broccoli (Limit to 3 times per week)	Beet greens
	Carrots, raw (Limit to 3 times per week)	Brussel sprouts
	Celery (Limit to 3 times per week)	Chinese cabbage
	Corn (Limit to 3 times per week)	Dried beans
	Cucumber, peeled	Dried peas
	Cabbage (except Chinese cabbage)	French fries
	Cauliflower	Potato
	Green beans	Pickles
	Eggplant	Olives
	Garlic	Sauerkraut
	Lettuce (1 cup per serving)	Split peas
	Onion	Sweet potato
	Pepper	Spinach
	Radish	Tomato
	Watercress	Tomato juice
	Zucchini	Tomato sauce
	Green peas (Limit to 3 times per week)	Winter squash (pumpkin, acorn butternut)
	Kale (Limit to 3 times per week)	Swiss Chard
	Mushrooms (Limit to 3 times per week)	Vegetables, canned
	Turnips (Limit to 3 times per week)	

Meat 1 – 2 oz. meat per serving (4-6 oz per day)- please speak with your renal dietitian to get guidelines regarding your protein intake	Beef Eggs Egg whites Fish Salt-free canned tuna Salmon Game Lamb Pork Poultry Tofu (3 ½ oz per serving)	Processed meats Bacon Deli meats Hot dogs Sausages
Fats	Butter Canola oil Mayonnaise Margarine, unsalted Olive oil Salad dressing, low sodium	Bacon fat Nuts Salted butter Salted margarine Salty salad dressings
Fluids	Coffee Tea Fruit ice Fruit flavored drink Lemonade Water	Iced teas with phosphorus additives Coconut water Cola beverages Dark-colored soda Beer

Other	Allspice	Chocolate
	Cinnamon	Ketchup
	Dill	Molasses
	Garlic powder	Mustard
	Onion powder	Salt
	Honey	Salt substitute
	Mints	Seasoning with salt
	Nutmeg	Soy sauce
	Parsley	Microwaveable meals
	Black pepper	
	Rosemary	
	Sage	
	Sugar	
	Syrup	
	Oregano	
	Thyme	

Conclusion

Put simply, anyone with weak kidneys should be on the renal diet. Apart from strictly following the list of foods provided under the auspices of these diets, certain foods should also not be eaten at all when on the renal diet.

The nature of the renal diet is very significant in the effective management of blood pressure in patients, along with the reduction of serum cholesterol levels. The renal diet is also known to improve the bio-profile of the plasma lipid.

Risk factors such as increased asymmetric dimethylarginine levels, stress due to oxidation, inflammation, can be addressed, and the effects reversed when the kidney diet is followed judiciously. However, early checks and measures often go a long way to determine the survival of the major people at risk.

Close work with medical professionals will ensure the success of the renal diet in most cases.

Veggie Eggs

Sodium - 160.1mg; **Potassium** - 378.5mg; **Phosphorus** - 236.8mg

Check with a kidney doctor or dietitian for guidelines to adjust protein intake.

Prep Time:	10 m	Calories:	236
Cook Time:	10 m	Fat (g):	16.8
Total Time:	20 m	Protein (g):	14
Servings:	2	Carbs (g):	7.4

These veggies eggs are a delight to serve with crispy toasted bread slices in the morning.

Ingredients:

- Eggs   4
- Cauliflower   1 cup
- Garlic clove, minced   1
- Bell pepper, chopped   ¼ cup
- Onion, chopped   ¼ cup
- Black pepper   ¼ teaspoon
- Avocado oil   1 tablespoon
- Fresh parsley   For garnish
- Spring onion   For garnish

Instructions:

1. Beat eggs and mix with black pepper in a bowl.
2. Heat a greased skillet over medium heat.
3. Stir in onion, and bell peppers, then sauté until golden.
4. Add garlic, then sauté for 15 seconds.
5. Add cauliflower and cover to cook for 5 minutes on medium-low heat.
6. Pour in eggs and mix well vegetables. Cook for 3 minutes or until the eggs are ready.
7. Garnish with spring onion and parsley.
8. Serve warm.

Pineapple Chicken Enchiladas

Sodium - 160.5mg; **Potassium** - 324.2mg; **Phosphorus** - 130.1mg

Check with a kidney doctor or dietitian for guidelines to adjust protein intake.

Prep Time:	10 m	Calories:	164
Cook Time:	25 m	Fat (g):	1.8
Total Time:	35 m	Protein (g):	17.3
Servings:	6	Carbs (g):	18.8

You must have tried the chicken enchiladas, but this recipe has a pineapple chicken filling, which gives these enchiladas a whole new taste.

Ingredients:

- Chicken breasts, boneless, skinless, sliced   10 oz (283g)
- Green Chile Enchilada sauce   10 oz (283g)
- Water   2/3 cup
- Garlic clove, minced   1
- Pineapple   ½ cup
- Green onions, sliced   ½ cup
- Paprika   ¼ teaspoon
- Cayenne   ¼ teaspoon
- Cumin   ¼ teaspoon
- White corn tortillas   6
- Cilantro, chopped   ½ cup

Instructions:

1. Set oven to 350 degrees F (177 °C) and let preheat.
2. Cook the chicken strips with some cooking oil in a skillet over medium-high heat until golden brown.
3. Mix 2/3 cup of water with enchilada sauce in a small bowl.
4. Add 1/3 cup of enchilada sauce, ¼ cup of green onions, ½ cup of pineapple, garlic, cumin, paprika, and cayenne to the chicken.
5. Cook until the chicken is tender, then transfer to a bowl.
6. Warm tortillas in a large skillet and keep them on a working surface.
7. Divide the chicken-pineapple mixture at the center of all tortillas.
8. Roll the tortillas and place these rolls in a baking dish with their seam side down.
9. Now pour the remaining sauce on top and bake for 7 minutes in the oven.
10. Garnish enchiladas with cilantro and green onions, then serve.

Cabbage Slaw

Sodium – 38.7mg; **Potassium** - 252.6mg; **Phosphorus** - 31.1mg

Prep Time:	10 m	**Calories:**	93
Cook Time:	0 m	**Fat (g):**	7
Total Time:	10 m	**Protein (g):**	1.3
Servings:	6	**Carbs (g):**	8

Here comes a basic cabbage slaw with a refreshing blend of lime juice and cilantro; add carrots to the combination, and this slaw will be perfect for serving with every entrée.

Ingredients:

- Green cabbage, shredded   3 cups
- Red cabbage, shredded   2 cups
- Carrots, shredded   2 cups
- Cilantro, chopped   ½ cup
- Lime juice   4 tablespoons
- Olive oil   3 tablespoons

Instructions:

1. Toss all the cabbages, carrots, cilantro, lime juice, and olive oil in a salad bowl.
2. Serve.

Egg Muffin Cups

Sodium – 160.2mg; **Potassium** - 227.7mg; **Phosphorus** - 211.5mg

Check with a kidney doctor or dietitian for guidelines to adjust protein intake.

Prep Time:	15 m	Calories:	177
Cook Time:	30 m	Fat (g):	12.6
Total Time:	45 m	Protein (g):	12.9
Servings:	4 (3 muffins)	Carbs (g):	2.4

One word for these egg cups– flavorsome! Here is a smart way to incorporate eggs, carrots, squash, and red pepper all in one meal.

Ingredients:

- Carrot, shredded   1/3 cup
- Yellow squash, shredded   1/3 cup
- Red pepper, shredded   1/3 cup
- Olive oil   1 teaspoon
- Eggs   8
- Fresh herbs   1 tablespoon
- Whole green onions, thinly sliced   3
- Mayo   2 teaspoons

Instructions:

1. Set oven to 350 degrees F (177 °C) and let preheat.
2. Sauté all the veggies with oil in a suitable skillet until soft.
3. Beat eggs with mayonnaise in a bowl, then add green onions and herbs.
4. Mix and add vegetables, then stir well.
5. Divide this egg-veggie mixture into a 12-cup muffin pan.
6. Bake the egg muffins for 25 minutes in the oven at 350 F (177 °C).
7. Serve warm.

no more than
2 grams salt per day. = 775mg Sodium

Chicken Fajitas

Sodium – 140.6mg; **Potassium** - 165.5mg; **Phosphorus** - 98.3mg

Check with a kidney doctor or dietitian for guidelines to adjust protein intake.

Prep Time:	15 m	**Calories:**	178
Cook Time:	20 m	**Fat (g):**	7
Total Time:	35 m	**Protein (g):**	12
Servings:	8 (1 Fajitas)	**Carbs (g):**	17.5

Chicken fajitas are a delight for every dinner table- now, you can make delicious chicken fajitas with this basic kidney-friendly recipe.

Ingredients:

• Flour tortillas, 6-inch size	8
• Green pepper, chopped	¼ cup
• Red pepper, chopped	¼ cup
• Onion, chopped	½ cup
• Cilantro, chopped	½ cup *Corriander.*
• Canola oil	2 tablespoons
• Boneless chicken breasts, cut into small strips	12 oz. (340g)
• Black pepper	¼ teaspoon
• Chili powder	2 teaspoons
• Cumin	½ teaspoon
• Lemon juice	2 tablespoons

Instructions:

1. Set oven to 300 degrees F (149 °C) and let preheat.
2. Wrap all the tortillas in a foil sheet and warm them for 10 minutes in the oven.
3. Sauté chicken with lemon juice, oil, and seasonings in a skillet for 5 minutes.
4. Stir in onion and peppers, then sauté for 5 minutes.
5. Add cilantro, then mix well.
6. Divide this chicken mixture into the tortillas and roll them.
7. Serve.

Vegetable Soup

Sodium – 76.3mg; **Potassium** - 248.9mg; **Phosphorus** - 29.7mg

Prep Time:	15 m	**Calories:**	55
Cook Time:	51 m	**Fat (g):**	2.4
Total Time:	1 h 6 m	**Protein (g):**	1.3
Servings:	6	**Carbs (g):**	7.7

I would recommend this vegetable soup to all not because it is tasty but because it is super healthy and loaded with so many nutrients and fibers.

Ingredients:

- Onion, medium, chopped   1
- Carrots, chopped   6
- Turnip, medium, chopped   1
- Celery sticks, chopped   2
- Garlic cloves, chopped   2
- Chicken broth (or Vegetable   5 cups
  Broth), low sodium
- Bay leaf   1
- Fresh thyme, chopped   1 teaspoon
- Black pepper   ¼ teaspoon
- Olive oil   1 tablespoon

Instructions:

1. Sauté onion, carrot, and turnip with oil in a skillet for 5 minutes.
2. Stir in garlic and celery, then sauté for 1 minute.
3. Add bay leaf, thyme, black pepper, and chicken broth.
4. Cover and cook the soup for 45 minutes on a simmer with occasional stirring.
5. Discard the bay leaf.
6. Let the soup cool for 5 minutes, then puree it by using an immersion blender until smooth.
7. Serve warm.

Omelet

Sodium – 195mg; **Potassium** - 300.4mg; **Phosphorus** - 220.6mg

Check with a kidney doctor or dietitian for guidelines to adjust protein intake.

Prep Time:	5 m	**Calories:**	302
Cook Time:	3 m	**Fat (g):**	25.4
Total Time:	8 m	**Protein (g):**	13.4
Servings:	1	**Carbs (g):**	5.3

Omelet is a must for every breakfast meal- So why not try this simple recipe full of nutrients.

Ingredients:

- Eggs   2
- Water   2 tablespoons
- Unsalted butter   1 tablespoon
- Vegetables, kidney-friendly   ½ cup

Instructions:

1. Beat eggs with water in a bowl.
2. Grease a 10-inch pan with butter and heat it until it sizzles.
3. Pour in the eggs and cook until the eggs are set.
4. Add veggies on top of the omelet.
5. Fold the omelet in half and slide it onto a plate.
6. Serve.

Roasted Garlic Cauliflower

Sodium – 45.5mg; **Potassium** - 451.6mg; **Phosphorus** - 71.5mg

Prep Time:	10 m	Calories:	133
Cook Time:	40 m	Fat (g):	10.6
Total Time:	50 m	Protein (g):	3.1
Servings:	4	Carbs (g):	8.8

If you just can't get enough of the cauliflower, then try this easy and quick roasted cauliflower recipe to serve at the table.

Ingredients:

- Minced garlic   2 tablespoons
- Olive oil   3 tablespoons
- Cauliflower, florets   1 large head
- Black pepper   To taste
- Parsley, chopped   1 tablespoon

Instructions:

1. Set oven to 400 degrees F (204 °C) and let preheat.
2. Grease a large casserole dish with cooking oil.
3. Mix olive oil with garlic in a bowl and toss in cauliflower and black pepper.
4. Stir and spread the mixture in the casserole dish.
5. Bake the cauliflower for 40 minutes until golden brown.
6. Sprinkle parsley on top.
7. Serve warm.

Cinnamon Rice Pudding

Sodium – 66.3mg; **Potassium** - 129.4mg; **Phosphorus** - 147.5mg

Prep Time:	5 m	Calories:	154
Cook Time:	20 m	Fat (g):	5.6
Total Time:	25 m	Protein (g):	2.5
Servings:	4	Carbs (g):	23.6

You will not believe how amazing this rice pudding tastes when served at breakfast or as a light dessert.

Ingredients:

- Almond milk   1 ½ cups
- White rice   9 oz (255g)
- Water   3 cups
- Ground cinnamon   2 teaspoons
- Desiccated coconut   1 oz (28g)

Instructions:

1. Add rice and boiling water to a saucepan and cook on a simmer until rice is soft.
2. When the rice has absorbed all the liquid, stir in milk and coconut, mix well and cook until it makes thick pudding.
3. Divide the pudding into the serving bowls.
4. Garnish with cinnamon powder.
5. Serve.

Egg-in-a-Hole

Sodium – 173mg; **Potassium** - 94.7mg; **Phosphorus** - 119.9mg

Prep Time:	5 m	**Calories:**	223
Cook Time:	2 m	**Fat (g):**	17
Total Time:	7 m	**Protein (g):**	7.9
Servings:	1	**Carbs (g):**	9.6

Here is a creative way to enjoy the same old bread slice with egg and butter.

Ingredients:

- Bread   1 slice
- Butter   1 tablespoon
- Egg   1
- Black pepper   To taste

Instructions:

1. Place the bread slice on the working surface and cut a hole at the center using a cookie cutter.
2. Add butter to a skillet and place it over medium-low heat.
3. Place the holed bread in the skillet and crack one egg into its hole.
4. Cook for 1 minute, then sprinkle black pepper on top.
5. Flip it over and cook 1 minute more.
6. Serve immediately.

Cream of Mushroom Soup

Sodium – 162.8mg; **Potassium** - 123.6mg; **Phosphorus** - 53.8mg

Prep Time:	10 m	**Calories:**	208
Cook Time:	15 m	**Fat (g):**	18.3
Total Time:	25 m	**Protein (g):**	2.2
Servings:	2	**Carbs (g):**	10.1

Ingredients:

• Unsalted butter	3 tablespoons
• Onion, minced	¼ cup
• Mushrooms, minced (1 cup per week per person)	¼ cup
• All-purpose flour	2 ½ tablespoons
• Chicken broth, low sodium	½ cup
• Almond milk	½ cup
• Black pepper	To taste

Instructions:

1. Sauté onion with butter in a 10-inch skillet until soft.
2. Stir in mushrooms and sauté for 5 minutes.
3. Sprinkle the flour over the veggies and sauté for 1-2 minutes.
4. Pour in milk and broth, then mix until smooth and lump-free.
5. Cook for 5 minutes with occasional stirring.
6. Serve warm.

Apple Filled Crepes

__Sodium__ – 87mg; __Potassium__ - 268.5mg; __Phosphorus__ - 118mg

Prep Time:	10 m	Calories:	544
Cook Time:	10 m	Fat (g):	30
Total Time:	20 m	Protein (g):	6.8
Servings:	6	Carbs (g):	64

Who does not love to have apple-filled crepes in the morning? If you do like the idea of having loaded crepes in breakfast, then try this recipe.

Ingredients:

• Egg yolks	4
• Whole eggs	2
• Sugar	½ cup
• Flour	1 cup
• Olive oil	¼ cup
• Almond milk	2 cups
• Apples, peeled, cored, and sliced	4
• Brown sugar	½ cup
• Cinnamon	½ teaspoon
• Nutmeg	½ teaspoon
• Unsalted butter	½ cup

Instructions:

1. Beat egg yolks with milk, oil, flour, sugar, and whole eggs in a bowl until lump-free.
2. Take a greased skillet, place it over medium heat, and when hot, spoon batter in it, 3-4 tablespoons per pancake, and then cook for 1 minute per side until golden.
3. Transfer the crepes to a plate and keep them aside.
4. Mix brown sugar, butter, and apples in a skillet.
5. Stir in nutmeg and cinnamon, then sauté until the apples are soft.
6. Divide the apple filling into each crepe and roll them.
7. Serve!

Deviled Eggs

Sodium – 124mg; **Potassium** - 73mg; **Phosphorus** - 90mg

Prep Time:	5 m	Calories:	101
Cook Time:	0 m	Fat (g):	7
Total Time:	5 m	Protein (g):	6
Servings:	4	Carbs (g):	2

No snack table seems complete without a platter of deviled eggs served on it! This time you can enjoy some creamy deviled egg with a tangy twist of paprika and mustard.

Ingredients:

• Eggs, hard-boiled, peeled	4
• Light mayonnaise	2 tablespoons
• Dry mustard	½ teaspoon
• Apple cider vinegar	½ teaspoon
• Onion, chopped	1 tablespoon
• Ground black pepper	¼ teaspoon
• Paprika	½ teaspoon

Instructions:

1. Slice the peeled eggs in half lengthwise.
2. Remove the egg yolks from the egg whites and transfer the yolks to a small bowl.
3. Place the egg whites on the serving plate.
4. Mash yolks and add black pepper, mayonnaise, vinegar, onion, and mustard, then mix well.
5. Divide this mixture into the egg whites.
6. Garnish with paprika, then serve.

Apple Pineapple Marshmallow Coleslaw

Sodium – 95.5mg; **Potassium** - 366mg; **Phosphorus** - 32.7mg

Prep Time:	15 m	Calories:	274
Cook Time:	0 m	Fat (g):	11
Total Time:	15 m	Protein (g):	2
Servings:	4	Carbs (g):	45.5

You must have tried cabbage coleslaws before, but this one tastes different as it is loaded with pineapple, apple, and marshmallows.

Ingredients:

• Pineapple chunks, drained	1 (8-oz./227g) can
• Apple, cored and chopped	1
• Red cabbage, shredded	2 cups
• Green cabbage, shredded	2 cups
• Celery, sliced	1 stalk
• Mini marshmallows	1 cup
• Mayonnaise	1 cup
• Apple cider vinegar	2 tablespoons
• White sugar	2 tablespoons
• Black pepper	½ teaspoon

Instructions:

1. Mix pineapple, apple, cabbage, celery, and marshmallows in a large bowl.
2. Mix the rest of the ingredients in a small bowl and pour over the prepared salad.
3. Stir well and cover to refrigerate for 1 hour.
4. Serve.

Chicken Fusilli Salad

Sodium – 56.5mg; **Potassium** - 346.5mg; **Phosphorus** - 154.1mg

Prep Time:	2 h 15 m	Calories:	442
Cook Time:	0 m	Fat (g):	29
Total Time:	2 h 15 m	Protein (g):	18
Servings:	4	Carbs (g):	27.6

Pasta lovers! Get ready to satisfy your pasta craving with this effortless pasta and chicken salad, which is seasoned with sweet and savory basil mixed dressing.

Ingredients:

Dressing

• Olive oil	½ cup
• Vinegar	¼ cup
• White pepper	½ teaspoon
• Basil	¼ teaspoon
• Sugar	1 teaspoon

Salad

• Cooked fusilli pasta	3 cups
• Cooked chicken, diced	8 oz. (227g)
• Frozen peas, defrosted	½ cup
• Carrot, chopped	1
• Red pepper, chopped	¼ cup
• Asparagus, ends removed, cut into 2-inch pieces	½ bunch

Instructions:

1. Mix olive oil, vinegar, white pepper, basil, and sugar in a salad bowl.
2. Cover and refrigerate the dressing for 2 hours.
3. Add pasta, chicken, peas, carrot, red pepper, and asparagus to the dressing.
4. Mix well and serve.

Lemon Poppy Seed Muffins

Sodium – 135mg; **Potassium** - 79.5mg; **Phosphorus** - 86.5mg

Prep Time:	15 m	Calories:	228.5
Cook Time:	20 m	Fat (g):	11.1
Total Time:	35 m	Protein (g):	4.1
Servings:	12	Carbs (g):	29.2

These lemon poppy seed muffins are a delight in the morning or as an evening snack.

Ingredients:

• Sugar	2/3 cup
• Grated zest and juice	1 lemon
• All-purpose flour	2 cups
• Baking powder	2 teaspoons
• Baking soda	¼ teaspoon
• Sour cream	3/4 cup
• Eggs	2
• Vanilla extract	1 teaspoon
• Unsalted butter, melted and cooled	½ cup
• Poppy seeds	2 tablespoons

Instructions:

1. Set oven to 400 degrees F (204 °C) and let preheat.
2. Take a 12 cup muffin pan and grease it with butter.
3. Mix sugar and lemon zest in a bowl.
4. Stir in baking powder, flour, and baking soda and mix well.
5. Beat eggs, lemon juice, vanilla, sour cream, and butter in a bowl.
6. Stir in flour mixture and mix well until smooth.
7. Fold in poppy seeds, then mix well.
8. Divide this muffin batter into the muffin cups.
9. Bake the muffin for 20 minutes in the oven until golden brown.
10. Allow the muffins to cool and serve.

Grilled Salmon with Paprika & Parsley Sauce

Sodium – 87.7mg; **Potassium** - 449mg; **Phosphorus** - 317.5mg

Check with a kidney doctor or dietitian for guidelines to adjust protein intake.

Prep Time:	10 m	Calories:	333
Cook Time:	15 m	Fat (g):	20.3
Total Time:	25 m	Protein (g):	24.7
Servings:	4	Carbs (g):	11.7

Do you want to serve fancy and delicious seafood at the table? Then this grilled salmon recipe with a parsley sauce is perhaps the right fit for you.

Ingredients:

• Butter	3 oz (85g)
• Salmon fillets	1 lb (454g)
• All-purpose flour	2 oz (56g)
• Lemon juice	1 lemon
• Fresh parsley	2 tablespoons
• Paprika	1 teaspoon
• Garlic clove, chopped	1

Instructions:

1. Pat dry the fish and coat it with flour.
2. Add half of the butter to a skillet and melt it.
3. Pour this melted butter over the fish.
4. Add the coated fish with butter to the grill pan along with garlic and cook for 6 minutes per side.
5. Mix remaining butter with paprika, parsley, and lemon juice in a bowl.
6. Pour this sauce over the fish.
7. Serve warm.

Chicken Curry

Sodium – 36mg; **Potassium** - 295mg; **Phosphorus** - 172.5mg

Check with a kidney doctor or dietitian for guidelines to adjust protein intake.

Prep Time:	15 m	**Calories:**	157
Cook Time:	35 m	**Fat (g):**	7
Total Time:	50 m	**Protein (g):**	17
Servings:	6	**Carbs (g):**	2.8

Everyone loves to have classic chicken curry every once in a while, well now; you can enjoy it with this low-sodium recipe as well.

Ingredients:

• Chicken, boneless, diced	1 lb (454g)
• Garlic clove, crushed	1
• Onion, chopped	1
• Olive oil	1 tablespoon
• Water	1 cup
• Black pepper	¼ teaspoon
• Curry powder	1 tablespoon
• Flour	1 teaspoon
• Butter, unsalted	1 oz (28g)

Instructions:

1. Sauté garlic and onion with olive oil in a skillet until golden.
2. Add chicken cubes to the skillet and sauté until golden.
3. Mix flour with melted butter in another pan.
4. Stir in enough water until it makes a smooth paste.
5. Mix the remaining water with black pepper and curry powder in a bowl.
6. Pour this mixture into the flour mixture and mix well.
7. Pour this sauce into the chicken and cover to cook on a simmer for 20 minutes.
8. Mix well and serve warm with white rice.

Mashed Cauliflower

Sodium – 128.5mg; **Potassium** - 477.3mg; **Phosphorus** - 88.3mg

Prep Time:	15 m	**Calories:**	146
Cook Time:	12 m	**Fat (g):**	11.6
Total Time:	27 m	**Protein (g):**	4.2
Servings:	8	**Carbs (g):**	8.5

So, what if you can't have mashed potatoes on the menu! Now you can enjoy something healthier and creamier with this mashed cauliflower recipe.

Ingredients:

• Cauliflower, florets removed	2 medium heads
• Cream cheese, softened	6 oz (170g)
• Almond milk	1/3 cup
• Black pepper	To taste
• Chives, chopped	For garnish
• Unsalted butter	For serving

Instructions:

1. Boil cauliflower in a saucepan filled with water for 10 minutes, then drain.
2. Transfer the cauliflower to a bowl and mash with a potato masher until smooth.
3. Add milk, black pepper, and cream cheese, then mix well.
4. Garnish with chives and butter.
5. Serve.

Creamy Roasted Cauliflower Soup

Sodium – 51.7mg; **Potassium** - 379.3mg; **Phosphorus** - 52.03mg

Prep Time:	15 m	Calories:	141.1
Cook Time:	55 m	Fat (g):	10.8
Total Time:	1 h 10 m	Protein (g):	2.3
Servings:	6	Carbs (g):	10.1

This roasted cauliflower soup has no parallel in taste. The creamy soup is served with roasted cauliflower florets on top.

Ingredients:

- Cauliflower, cut into florets   1 large head
- Olive oil   3 tablespoons

- Red onion, medium, chopped   1
- Garlic cloves, minced   2
- Vegetable broth, low sodium   4 cups
- Unsalted butter   2 tablespoons
- Fresh lemon juice   1 tablespoon
- Ground nutmeg   ¼ teaspoon
- Fresh parsley, chopped   2 tablespoons

Instructions:

1. Set oven to 425 degrees F (218 °C) and let preheat.
2. Layer a baking sheet with a parchment sheet.
3. Toss cauliflower with 2 tablespoons of olive oil in a bowl and spread on the baking sheet.
4. Bake cauliflower florets for 35 minutes in the oven, tossing them halfway through.
5. Sauté onion with 1 tablespoon of olive oil in a soup pot for 5 minutes until soft.
6. Add garlic and sauté for 30 seconds, then pour in broth.
7. When the cauliflower is finished baking, keep some cauliflower florets aside for serving.
8. Add the remaining cauliflower florets to the soup pot and cook on a simmer for 20 minutes with occasional stirring.
9. When done, remove the soup pot from the heat and let the soup cool for 2 minutes.
8. Add butter, lemon juice, and nutmeg, then puree the soup using an immersion blender until smooth.
10. Divide the soup among the bowls and garnish with cauliflower florets and parsley.
11. Serve.

Chicken Fillet with Cranberry Sauce

Sodium – 39.2mg; **Potassium** - 355.7mg; **Phosphorus** - 176.7mg

Check with a kidney doctor or dietitian for guidelines to adjust protein intake.

Prep Time:	10 m	**Calories:**	226.3
Cook Time:	22 m	**Fat (g):**	7.1
Total Time:	32 m	**Protein (g):**	17.6
Servings:	8	**Carbs (g):**	16.9

Here comes a chicken cranberry sauce recipe with a refreshing blend of cranberries with maple syrup; add chicken to the combination, and this will be the perfect meal to serve.

Ingredients:

• Chicken breasts, boneless	1 ½ lbs (680g)
• Black pepper	To taste
• Olive oil	3 tablespoons
• Yellow onion, diced	1
• Dry red wine	1 cup
• Pure maple syrup	½ cup
• Cranberries	½ cup
• Cornstarch	4 teaspoons
• Water	4 teaspoons

Instructions:

1. Season chicken breasts with black pepper.
2. Sauté chicken with 2 tablespoons of olive oil in a skillet for 5 minutes per side until golden brown, then transfer to a plate.
3. Saute onions with oil in a saucepan for 5 minutes.
4. Stir in cranberries, syrup, and wine, then bring to a boil over high heat.
5. Reduce heat and cook for 5 minutes with occasional stirring.
6. Mix cornstarch with water in a small bowl.
7. Stir in cornstarch mixture, and continue cooking for 1 minute.
8. When done, pour the sauce over the chicken breasts and serve.

Simple Chicken Soup

Sodium – 79.3mg; **Potassium** - 398.6mg; **Phosphorus** - 129.5mg

Check with a kidney doctor or dietitian for guidelines to adjust protein intake.

Prep Time:	10 m	Calories:	105.5
Cook Time:	50 m	Fat (g):	1.6
Total Time:	1 hour	Protein (g):	14.3
Servings:	8	Carbs (g):	7.6

A healthy chicken soup cooked with veggies and low-sodium ingredients is highly rec-ommended for all those who are healing- so here is your chance to try one!

42 gms
per day

Ingredients:

- Chicken breasts, skinless   1 lb (454g)
- Chicken broth, low sodium   4 cups
- Water   4 cups
- Carrots, sliced   2
- Celery, sliced   2 stalks
- Onion, medium, chopped   1
- Bay leaf   1
- White rice   ½ cup
- Chopped parsley   2 tablespoons

Instructions:

1. Add chicken to a pot and fill it with water and broth.
2. Place the pot on medium-high heat and cook for 20 minutes.
3. Remove the chicken using a slotted spoon.
4. Add the bay leaf, onion, celery, and carrots to the broth and cook for 10 minutes.
5. Stir in rice and cook for 15 minutes.
6. Shred the chicken.
7. When the rice is done, add the chicken to the broth and cook for 1 minute.
8. Stir in parsley and serve.

Baked Cod

Sodium – 64mg; **Potassium** - 477mg; **Phosphorus** - 231mg

Check with a kidney doctor or dietitian for guidelines to adjust protein intake.

Prep Time:	5 m	Calories:	153.7
Cook Time:	12 m	Fat (g):	7.5
Total Time:	17 m	Protein (g):	19.8
Servings:	4	Carbs (g):	0.3

A freshly baked cod serving in a platter is a site to see! Well, this baked cod is also bliss for your taste buds due to its refreshing lemon flavors.

Ingredients:

• Cod fillets, rinsed and pat dry	1 lb (454g)
• Lemon juice	1 tablespoon
• Cayenne pepper	½ teaspoon
• Olive oil	2 tablespoons
• Chopped parsley	1 tablespoon

Instructions:

1. Set oven to 400 degrees F (204 °C) and let preheat.
2. Place the cod fillets on a baking sheet.
3. Mix olive oil with cayenne pepper and lemon juice and pour over the fish.
4. Bake the cod for 12 minutes in the preheated oven.
5. Garnish the fish with parsley.
6. Serve.

Asian Chicken Lettuce Wrap

Sodium – 203.7mg; **Potassium** - 423.3mg; **Phosphorus** - 124.5mg

Check with a kidney doctor or dietitian for guidelines to adjust protein intake.

Prep Time:	10 m	**Calories:**	131.2
Cook Time:	10 m	**Fat (g):**	6.7
Total Time:	20 m	**Protein (g):**	11.1
Servings:	8	**Carbs (g):**	7.3

Ingredients:

• Olive oil	1 tablespoon
• Ground chicken	1 lb (454g)
• Garlic cloves, minced	2
• Onion, diced	1
• Hoisin sauce (Be careful, 130 Sodium per serving)	¼ cup
• Rice wine vinegar	1 tablespoon
• Ginger, grated	1 tablespoon
• Sriracha	1 tablespoon
• Green onions, thinly sliced	2
• Black pepper	To taste
• Lettuce	1 head

Instructions:

1. Add olive oil to a saucepan, then heat it on medium-high heat.
2. Sauté chicken over medium-high heat for 5 minutes.
3. Stir in Sriracha, ginger, rice wine vinegar, hoisin sauce, onion, garlic, and cook for 2 minutes.
4. Add green onions, then sauté for 2 minutes.
5. Season with black pepper, then mix well.
6. Place the lettuce leaves on the serving plates.
7. Divide the chicken filling in the lettuce leaves.
8. Serve.

Chilli Tuna Spaghetti

Sodium – 50mg; **Potassium** - 203mg; **Phosphorus** - 163.5mg

Prep Time:	10 m	Calories:	454
Cook Time:	10 m	Fat (g):	9.3
Total Time:	20 m	Protein (g):	27.7
Servings:	4	Carbs (g):	64.2

Tuna served with spaghetti is one of the great serving for every dinner table. Try this combination with this easy recipe.

Ingredients:

• Tuna, salt-free	2 tins (10 oz(283g))
• Spaghetti	12 oz (340g)
• Fresh parsley, chopped	1 bunch
• Garlic cloves, crushed	2
• Juice of lemon	½ lemon
• Dried chili flakes	2 teaspoons
• Black pepper	To taste
• Olive oil	2 tablespoons

Instructions:

1. Cook spaghetti according to the package instructions.
2. Sauté garlic with 1 tablespoon of olive oil in a skillet until golden brown.
3. Stir in tuna, chili flakes, lemon juice, and 1 tablespoon of olive oil.
4. Drain the pasta and add to the tuna.
5. Stir in black pepper and parsley and mix well.
6. Serve.

Carrot Pineapple Salad

Sodium – 61.5mg; **Potassium** - 374.5mg; **Phosphorus** - 50.3mg

Prep Time:	15 m	Calories:	141.2
Cook Time:	0 m	Fat (g):	0.5
Total Time:	15 m	Protein (g):	1.9
Servings:	4	Carbs (g):	34.4

This pineapple and carrot salad are a pleasing surprise for all those who enjoy having juicy salads full of nutrients and fibers.

Ingredients:

- Carrots, peeled, shredded — 2 cups
- Small pineapple chunks — 2 cups
- Celery, shredded — ½ cup
- Dairy-free plain yogurt — ¼ cup
- Juice of lime — ½ lime
- Apple cider vinegar — 1 teaspoon
- Ground turmeric — ¼ teaspoons

Instructions:

1. Add the carrot to a salad bowl.
2. Toss in pineapple, celery and mix well.
3. Whisk yogurt with lime juice, apple cider vinegar, and turmeric in a small bowl.
4. Add this dressing to the salad and mix well.
5. Serve.

Chicken Fried Rice

<u>Sodium</u> – 70.5mg; <u>Potassium</u> - 342.6mg; <u>Phosphorus</u> - 194.8mg

<u>Check with a kidney doctor or dietitian for guidelines to adjust protein intake.</u>

Prep Time:	20 m	Calories:	251.4
Cook Time:	25 m	Fat (g):	8.7
Total Time:	45 m	Protein (g):	19.5
Servings:	10	Carbs (g):	22.3

No menu is complete without a bowl of colorful fried rice.

Ingredients:

• Olive oil	4 tablespoons
• Chicken breasts	1 ½ lb (680g)
• Black pepper	To taste
• Onion, chopped	1
• Carrots, peeled and diced	2
• Garlic cloves, minced	3
• Ginger, minced	1 tablespoon
• Cooked white rice	4 cups
• Frozen peas, defrosted	½ cup
• Eggs, beaten	3
• Green onions, sliced	2

Instructions:

1. Season chicken breasts with black pepper.
2. Sauté chicken with 2 tablespoons of olive oil in a skillet for 5 minutes per side until golden brown.
3. Remove the chicken from the skillet and dice it.
4. Sauté carrots and onion with 1 tablespoon of olive oil in a skillet for 5 minutes.
5. Stir in ginger and garlic, then sauté for 1 minute.
6. Add peas and rice and cook for 2 minutes.
7. Push the mixture aside and add the remaining olive oil at the center.
8. Pour in beaten eggs and cook until set, then mix well with rice.
9. Add in chicken, green onions, and stir well to combine.
10. Serve.

Blueberry Muffins

Sodium – 141.3mg; **Potassium** - 67.3mg; **Phosphorus** - 66.2mg

Prep Time:	15 m	Calories:	266.8
Cook Time:	20 m	Fat (g):	10
Total Time:	35 m	Protein (g):	3.5
Servings:	8	Carbs (g):	41.5

Ingredients:

- All-purpose flour   1 ½ cups
- Granulated sugar   3/4 cup
- Baking powder   2 teaspoons
- Canola oil   1/3 cup
- Egg, large   1
- Almond milk   ½ cup
- Vanilla extract   1 ½ teaspoon
- Fresh blueberries   8 oz (227g)

Instructions:

1. Set oven to 400 degrees F (204 °C) and let preheat.
2. Line a muffin pan with paper liners.
3. Mix flour, baking powder, and sugar in a large bowl.
4. Beat egg with milk and oil in a mixing bowl.
5. Add the egg mixture to the flour mixture and stir in vanilla extract, then mix well until it makes a smooth batter.
6. Fold in berries and mix evenly, then divide into the muffin cups.
7. Bake these muffins for 20 minutes in the oven.
8. Allow the muffins to cool and then serve.

Pineapple Salsa

Sodium – 2mg; **Potassium** - 118.7mg; **Phosphorus** - 8mg

Prep Time:	10 m	Calories:	29
Cook Time:	0 m	Fat (g):	0.1
Total Time:	10 m	Protein (g):	0.5
Servings:	4	Carbs (g):	7.3

Juicy and sweet- this pineapple salsa is a must to have on your salsa menu so that you could enjoy a whole new blend of flavors.

Ingredients:

- Canned juice-packed pineapple   10 oz (283g)
- Red onion, chopped   ¼ cup
- Garlic clove, minced   1
- Jalapeno pepper, chopped   1 tablespoon
- Cilantro, chopped   2 tablespoons

HoT

Instructions:

1. Mix pineapple with jalapeno, garlic, onion, and cilantro in a salad bowl.
2. Serve.

Garlic Roasted Radishes

Sodium – 45mg; **Potassium** - 275mg; **Phosphorus** - 26.4mg

Prep Time:	10 m	Calories:	55.5
Cook Time:	30 m	Fat (g):	3.9
Total Time:	40 m	Protein (g):	0.9
Servings:	4	Carbs (g):	4.6

Garlic roasted radishes are tempting for all vegans!

Ingredients:

Wind!!

• Radishes, halved	1 lb (454g)
• Melted ghee	1 tablespoon
• Black pepper	½ teaspoon
• Garlic cloves, minced	3
• Dried parsley	½ teaspoon

Instructions:

1. Set oven to 425 degrees F (218 °C) and let preheat.
2. Toss radishes with black pepper and melted ghee in a bowl.
3. Spread the radishes in a 9x13 inches baking dish.
4. Bake the radishes for 25 minutes in the oven and toss the radishes every 10 minutes.
5. Stir in garlic and parsley and bake for 5 minutes or until radishes are cooked through.
6. Serve.

Summer Radish Salad

Sodium – 26.2mg; **Potassium** - 253.6mg; **Phosphorus** - 34.2mg

Prep Time:	15 m	Calories:	156
Cook Time:	1 h 5 m	Fat (g):	13.7
Total Time:	1 h 20 m	Protein (g):	1.2
Servings:	4	Carbs (g):	8.4

Ingredients:

• Radishes, sliced	2 cups
• Red onion, sliced	1 cup
• Cucumber, sliced	1 cup
• Olive oil	¼ cup
• White wine vinegar	2 tablespoons
• Garlic clove, minced	1
• Sugar	½ teaspoon
• Leek, chopped	¼ cup
• Chives, chopped	¼ cup

Instructions:

1. In a large salad bowl, add radishes, cucumber slices, red onion, garlic, sugar, vinegar, and olive oil.
2. Mix well and cover to refrigerate for 1 hour.
3. Garnish with leek and chives.
4. Serve.

Stuffed Peppers

Sodium – 60.5mg; **Potassium** - 342.6mg; **Phosphorus** - 146.1mg

Check with a kidney doctor or dietitian for guidelines to adjust protein intake.

Prep Time:	10 m	Calories:	152.2
Cook Time:	45 m	Fat (g):	3.6
Total Time:	55 m	Protein (g):	13.8
Servings:	8	Carbs (g):	15.6

Ingredients:

• Bell peppers	4
• Ground beef	1 lb (454g)
• Unsalted butter	1 teaspoon
• Onion, chopped	¼ cup
• Mild salsa	3 tablespoons
• Herb seasoning, salt-free	1 teaspoon
• Cooked white rice	2 cups
• Water	½ cup
• Paprika	1 teaspoon
• Parsley	For garnish

Instructions:

1. Preheat oven to 350 F (177 °C).
2. Remove the top and seeds of the peppers.
3. Boil the peppers in a pot filled with boiling water for 5 minutes, then remove them using a slotted spoon.
4. Sauté ground beef with olive oil in a pan until brown, then transfer to a plate.
5. Sauté onion with 1 teaspoon of butter in a skillet until soft.
6. Add the ground beef, cooked rice, herb seasoning, paprika, and salsa, then mix well. Divide this mixture into the peppers.
7. Place the stuffed peppers in a baking dish and pour ½ cup of water into the dish.
8. Cover and bake the peppers for 30 minutes at 350 F (177 °C) in the oven.
9. Uncover the peppers and bake for 5 minutes in the oven.
10. Garnish with parsley and serve.

Tip: Cut stuffed peppers in half if you have protein restrictions.

Buckwheat with Mushrooms

Sodium – 5.5mg; **Potassium** - 297.3mg; **Phosphorus** - 140.6mg

Prep Time:	10 m	Calories:	167
Cook Time:	40 m	Fat (g):	6.9
Total Time:	50 m	Protein (g):	5.3
Servings:	6	Carbs (g):	23.9

This combination of buckwheat with mushrooms is something that you must not have tried before- so try this simple and quick recipe.

Ingredients:

- Uncooked buckwheat   1 cup
- Water   2 cups
- Mushrooms, chopped (1 cup per week   8 oz (227g)
  per person)
- Onion, medium, chopped   1
- Green onions, diced (for garnish)   1 cup
- Unsalted butter   3 tablespoons

Instructions:

1. Add buckwheat with water in a cooking pot, bring to a boil and cook on low heat for 25 minutes.
2. Sauté onions with butter in a pan until soft.
3. Add mushrooms and sauté until golden brown.
4. Stir in buckwheat and let it sit for 5 minutes.
5. Garnish with green onions and mix well.
6. Serve.

Apple Muffins

Sodium – 117mg; **Potassium** - 46mg; **Phosphorus** - 34mg

Prep Time:	15 m	Calories:	221.5
Cook Time:	20 m	Fat (g):	10
Total Time:	35 m	Protein (g):	2.7
Servings:	12	Carbs (g):	30.7

There is one word for these apple muffins- delicious! I am amazed to see how simple a recipe can give you such an epic blend of flavors.

Ingredients:

- Raw apple, diced   1 ½ cups
- Eggs   2
- Sugar   1 cup
- Canola oil   ½ cup
- Water   ¼ cup
- Vanilla   1 tablespoon
- All-purpose flour   1 ½ cups
- Baking soda   1 teaspoon
- Cinnamon   1 ½ teaspoon

Instructions:

1. Mix 1 teaspoon of sugar with ½ teaspoon of cinnamon in a small bowl.
2. Set oven to 400 degrees F (204 °C) and let preheat.
3. Line a muffin pan with paper liners.
4. Beat eggs in a suitable bowl, then add water, oil, vanilla, and remaining sugar.
5. Mix well, then slowly add baking soda, flour, and 1 teaspoon of cinnamon.
6. Stir well until the batter is lump-free and smooth.
7. Fold in apple pieces, mix and divide the batter into the muffin cups.
8. Sprinkle the cinnamon mixture on top and bake for 20 minutes in the oven.
9. Allow the muffins to cool and serve.

Scrambled Egg Toast

Sodium – 383.5mg(with feta cheese); **Potassium** - 81.6mg; **Phosphorus** - 163mg

Check with a kidney doctor or dietitian for guidelines to adjust protein intake.

Prep Time:	5 m	Calories:	211
Cook Time:	8 m	Fat (g):	12.1
Total Time:	13 m	Protein (g):	12
Servings:	2	Carbs (g):	14.1

A breakfast without scrambled eggs? No way! So, try this scrambled egg on toast to serve a nutritious meal in the morning.

Ingredients:

- White bread slices   2
- Butter   ½ tablespoon + for bread
- Eggs   2
- Feta cheese crumbles (optional) No.   ¼ cup
- Chopped parsley, chives   To garnish

Instructions:

1. Add the thin layer of butter on both sides of the bread slices.
2. Fry the bread slices in a skillet for 2 minutes per side until golden brown.
3. Transfer the bread slices to a plate.
4. Add ½ tablespoon of butter to a skillet and melt it over medium heat.
5. Beat eggs, pour into the skillet and add feta cheese on top.
6. Stir and cook the eggs for 4 minutes.
7. Divide the scrambled eggs on top of the bread slices.
8. Garnish with parsley and chives.
9. Serve warm.

Bagel with Cream Cheese and Salmon

Sodium – 310.7mg; **Potassium** - 153.6mg; **Phosphorus** - 111.6mg

Check with a kidney doctor or dietitian for guidelines to adjust protein intake.

Prep Time:	10 m	**Calories:**	297.4
Cook Time:	5 m	**Fat (g):**	14.4
Total Time:	15 m	**Protein (g):**	13.8
Servings:	4	**Carbs (g):**	29.2

The bagel with salmon and cream cheese is a perfect breakfast meal that we must try. It has a mix of crispy texture and earthy flavors.

Ingredients:

- White seeded bagels, halved — 4
- Smoked salmon slices — 4 oz (113g)
- Lemon juice — 1 tablespoon
- Cream cheese — 5 oz (142g)
- Dill, chopped — 1 teaspoon

Instructions:

1. Fry the bagel halves in a skillet until golden brown from both sides.
2. Season the smoked salmon with lemon juice in a bowl.
3. Spread cream cheese on top of toasted bagel bottoms.
4. Place the smoked salmon on top of the cream cheese and drizzle dill on top.
5. Set the top halves of the bagel on top.
6. Serve.

Easy Broccoli Soup

Sodium – 80.8mg; **Potassium** - 435.8mg; **Phosphorus** - 106.8mg

Prep Time:	10 m	Calories:	102.6
Cook Time:	20 m	Fat (g):	5.8
Total Time:	30 m	Protein (g):	5.6
Servings:	6	Carbs (g):	9.6

This basic broccoli soup is something that every health enthusiast would love to have once. Try this simple recipe to cook a warming bowl of green soup.

Ingredients:

• Olive oil	2 tablespoons
• Fresh broccoli, cut into florets (1 cup per week per person)	1 lb (454g)
• Onion, chopped	1
• Carrot, shredded	1
• Black pepper	To taste
• Chicken broth, low sodium	4 cups

Instructions:

1. Sauté onion and carrot with olive oil in a medium pot over medium-high heat for 5 minutes until soft.
2. Stir in black pepper, chicken broth, and broccoli, then boil.
3. Reduce its heat and cook for 15 minutes on a simmer.
4. Let the soup cool for 5 minutes, then puree it by using an immersion blender until smooth.
5. Serve warm.

Baked Tilapia

Sodium – 62.8mg; **Potassium** - 395.1mg; **Phosphorus** - 203.8mg

Check with a kidney doctor or dietitian for guidelines to adjust protein intake.

Prep Time:	10 m	Calories:	245
Cook Time:	12 m	Fat (g):	16.4
Total Time:	22 m	Protein (g):	22.2
Servings:	4	Carbs (g):	3.8

A warming platter of baked tilapia is all you need to make your dinner table look special.
In this recipe, the delicious tilapia is cooked with a tang glaze of butter.

Ingredients:

• Tilapia fillets	1 lb (454g)
• Black pepper	To taste
• Butter, melted	5 tablespoons
• Garlic cloves, minced	2
• Crushed red pepper flakes	¼ teaspoons
• Juice and zest of lemon	½ lemon
• Lemon, sliced	1
• Parsley, chopped	For garnish

Instructions:

1. Set oven to 400 degrees F (204 °C) and let preheat.
2. Rub the tilapia with black pepper and place them on a baking sheet.
3. Mix red pepper flakes, garlic, butter, lemon zest, and lemon juice in a bowl.
4. Pour this mixture over the tilapia and place the lemon slices on top.
5. Bake the tilapia for 12 minutes in the preheated oven.
6. When done, garnish with chopped parsley.
7. Serve warm.

Stuffed Cabbage Rolls

Sodium – 58.3mg; **Potassium** - 313.3mg; **Phosphorus** - 143.8mg

Check with a kidney doctor or dietitian for guidelines to adjust protein intake.

Prep Time:	10 m	Calories:	140.2
Cook Time:	1 h	Fat (g):	6.9
Total Time:	1 h 10 m	Protein (g):	13.7
Servings:	8	Carbs (g):	6.2

Are you ready to enjoy some crunchy, saucy, and loaded cabbage rolls? Well, here is a recipe to cook delicious cabbage rolls filled with beef and rice stuffing.

Ingredients:

- Water   ⅔ cup
- Uncooked white rice   ⅓ cup
- Cabbage leaves   8
- Lean ground beef Turkey.   1 lb (454g)
- Onion, chopped   ¼ cup
- Egg, beaten   1
- Ground black pepper   ¼ teaspoon
- Olive oil   2 tablespoons
- Carrot, shredded   1
- Onion, chopped   1

Instructions:

1. Boil water in a suitable saucepan and add rice.
2. Cover, reduce its heat, and cook for 20 minutes on a simmer.
3. In another pan, add cabbage leaves to boiling water for 4 minutes, then drain.
4. Mix ground beef with black pepper, egg, ¼ cup of onion, and cooked rice in a bowl.
5. Place the cabbage leaves on the working surface.
6. Divide the beef mixture on top of the cabbage leaves.
7. Roll and wrap the cabbage leaves around the filling, then secure them with a toothpick.
8. Place the cabbage rolls in the pan with their seam side down.
9. Pour in the water, cover, and bring to a boil.
10. Lower the heat and cook for 40 minutes on a simmer.
11. Meanwhile, sauté remaining onion and carrot with olive oil in a skillet over medium-high heat for 5 minutes until soft.
12. When the cabbage rolls are ready, spread the roasted onion and carrot over the cabbage rolls.
13. Serve.

Beef Burritos

Sodium – 284.6mg; **Potassium** - 356.6mg; **Phosphorus** - 214.6mg

Check with a kidney doctor or dietitian for guidelines to adjust protein intake.

Prep Time:	10 m	**Calories:**	238.8
Cook Time:	20 m	**Fat (g):**	6.5
Total Time:	30 m	**Protein (g):**	20
Servings:	6	**Carbs (g):**	24.7

Ingredients:

- Onion, chopped   ¼ cup
- Red bell pepper, chopped   ½ cup
- Lean ground beef   1 lb (454g)
- Black pepper   ¼ teaspoon
- Ground cumin   ¼ teaspoon
- Flour tortillas   6

Instructions:

1. Sauté beef in a skillet until brown, then transfer to a bowl.
2. Add onion, red bell pepper to a greased skillet and sauté for 3 minutes until soft.
3. Stir in cumin, black pepper, and return the beef.
4. Mix and cook for 5 minutes on low heat.
5. Divide this beef mixture into tortillas and roll them in burrito style.
6. Serve.

Shrimp Fried Rice

Sodium – 264.8mg; **Potassium** - 132.6mg; **Phosphorus** - 184.5mg

Check with a kidney doctor or dietitian for guidelines to adjust protein intake.

Prep Time:	20 m	**Calories:**	255.3
Cook Time:	20 m	**Fat (g):**	11.7
Total Time:	40 m	**Protein (g):**	11
Servings:	6	**Carbs (g):**	25.5

Here comes a loaded fried rice recipe that is not only full of enticing flavors but it is equally nutritious and healthy.

Ingredients:

- Raw shrimp, shelled and deveined   8 oz (227g)
- Black pepper   To taste
- Cornstarch   ½ teaspoon
- Canola oil   3 tablespoons
- Eggs, beaten   3
- Green onion, minced   2 stalks
- Cooked white rice   3 cups
- Frozen peas and carrots, defrosted   ½ cup
- Sesame oil   1 teaspoon

Instructions:

1. Mix shrimp with cornstarch and black pepper in a medium bowl.
2. Cover shrimp and let it sit for 10 minutes.
3. Sauté shrimp with 1 tablespoon of canola oil in a skillet for 30 seconds, then flip them, and cook for 30 seconds more or until they are cooked through. Transfer the shrimp to a bowl.
4. Pour more oil into the same skillet.
5. Beat eggs in a bowl and pour into the skillet.
6. Stir, cook and scramble the eggs until set, then transfer to the shrimp.
7. Sauté rice and green onions with remaining oil for 3 minutes with occasional stirring.
8. Add in sesame oil, shrimp with eggs, peas, and carrots, and stir well.
9. Cook for 2 minutes and serve.

Zucchini Pancakes

Sodium – 166.2mg; **Potassium** - 314.6mg; **Phosphorus** - 127.6mg

Prep Time:	10 m	**Calories:**	124.2
Cook Time:	8 m	**Fat (g):**	5.7
Total Time:	18 m	**Protein (g):**	5.7
Servings:	4	**Carbs (g):**	13.2

Ingredients:

- Zucchini _courgett_   2
- Red onion, grated   2 tablespoons
- Eggs, lightly beaten   2
- All-purpose flour   6 tablespoons
- Baking powder   1 teaspoon
- Black pepper   ½ teaspoon
- Unsalted butter   1 tablespoon

Instructions:

1. Grate the zucchini into a suitable bowl.
2. Add eggs, onion, black pepper, baking powder, and flour.
3. Mix well and keep this zucchini mixture aside.
4. Set a sauté pan over medium heat and add 1 tablespoon of butter to melt and let it heat.
5. Spread a spoonful zucchini mixture into the pan and cook for 2 minutes per side.
6. Transfer the pancake to a plate and cook more pancakes.
7. Serve.

Shrimp and Broccoli Fettuccine

Sodium – 250.6mg; **Potassium** - 224.7mg; **Phosphorus** - 199.3mg

Check with a kidney doctor or dietitian for guidelines to adjust protein intake.

Prep Time:	15 m	Calories:	233.5
Cook Time:	20 m	Fat (g):	11.8
Total Time:	35 m	Protein (g):	12.9
Servings:	4	Carbs (g):	18.6

Enjoy the same old Fettucine with a nutritious combination of veggies and shrimp, and try this simple and quick recipe.

Ingredients:

• Fettuccine, uncooked	4 oz (113g)
• Broccoli florets (1 cup per week per person)	2 cups
• Frozen medium shrimp	3/4 lb (340g)
• Garlic clove, minced	1
• Cream cheese	6 oz (170g)
• Garlic powder	½ teaspoon
• Lemon juice	¼ cup
• Ground peppercorns	3/4 teaspoon
• Half & half creamer	¼ cup

Instructions:

1. Cook fettuccine according to the package instructions without using salt.
2. Drain and rinse the pasta in a colander, then keep it aside.
3. Boil broccoli in a pot filled with water for 3 minutes, then drain.
4. Sauté shrimp with garlic in a non-stick skillet for 3 minutes.
5. Add half and half, peppercorns, lemon juice, garlic powder, and cream cheese.
6. Mix and cook for 2 minutes, then toss in the pasta.
7. Serve.

Baked Tofu

Sodium – 182.5mg(with soy sauce); **Potassium** - 220.4mg; **Phosphorus** - 102.5mg

Prep Time:	20 m	Calories:	105.2
Cook Time:	30 m	Fat (g):	6.2
Total Time:	50 m	Protein (g):	7.7
Servings:	4	Carbs (g):	4.5

The low-sodium oven-baked tofu is known for its crisp and amazing flavors.

Ingredients:

- Tofu   1 block (15 oz (425g))
- Olive oil   1 tablespoon
- Soy sauce, low-sodium(optional)   1 tablespoon
- Cornstarch   1 tablespoon

Instructions:

1. Set oven to 400 degrees F (204 °C) and let preheat.
2. Layer a baking sheet with parchment paper.
3. Slice the tofu block into 3 slabs and pile up these slabs on top of one another.
4. Cut the slabs into 3 columns lengthwise and then slice 5 rows.
5. Place the tofu cubes between two heavy plates, and leave for 10 minutes to remove the excess liquid.
6. Place the tofu in a bowl and add olive oil, soy sauce, and cornstarch.
7. Mix well to coat the cubes, then spread the cubes on the baking sheet.
8. Bake the tofu for 30 minutes, tossing halfway through.
9. Serve.

Cauliflower Rice

Sodium – 62.2mg; **Potassium** - 480.1mg; **Phosphorus** - 70.8mg

Prep Time:	10 m	Calories:	67.7
Cook Time:	10 m	Fat (g):	1.7
Total Time:	20 m	Protein (g):	4.2
Servings:	4	Carbs (g):	11.8

Ingredients:

- Head of cauliflower   1
- Olive oil   1 teaspoon
- Scallions, chopped   ½ cup
- Lime juice   ½ lime
- Black pepper   To taste

Instructions:

1. Add cauliflower to a food processor and pulse to rice the veggies.
2. Take a skillet, and then heat olive oil over medium heat.
3. Sauté cauliflower rice with scallions in a skillet for 5 minutes.
4. Season with black pepper and drizzle lime juice over the cauliflower rice.
5. Serve.

Ground Beef Soup

Sodium – 115.5mg; **Potassium** - 448.6mg; **Phosphorus** - 225.8mg

Check with a kidney doctor or dietitian for guidelines to adjust protein intake.

Prep Time:	10 m	Calories:	222.3
Cook Time:	40 m	Fat (g):	6.9
Total Time:	50 m	Protein (g):	19.8
Servings:	6	Carbs (g):	19.2

A warming bowl of ground beef soup always seems irresistible! This one tastes great due to an amazing mix of veggies with different seasonings.

Ingredients:

- Lean ground beef   1 lb. (454g)
- Onion, chopped   ½ cup
- Lemon pepper seasoning   2 teaspoons
- Beef broth, low sodium   1 cup
- Water   2 cups
- White rice, uncooked   1/3 cup
- Frozen mixed vegetables, defrosted   3 cups
- Sour cream   1 tablespoon
- Olive oil   1 tablespoon

Instructions:

1. Sauté ground beef and onion with olive oil in a large saucepan until brown.
2. Stir in rice, vegetables, water, broth, seasoning.
3. Cook this mixture on high heat until it boils.
4. Reduce its heat to medium-low heat, then cover to cook for 30 minutes.
5. Remove the soup from the heat.
6. Add the sour cream and serve.

Buffalo Cauliflower Wings

Sodium – 87.6mg; **Potassium** - 339.3mg; **Phosphorus** - 54.3mg

Prep Time:	15 m	**Calories:**	134.8
Cook Time:	36 m	**Fat (g):**	3.2
Total Time:	51 m	**Protein (g):**	3.6
Servings:	6	**Carbs (g):**	20.1

These buffalo cauliflower wings are another way to enjoy low-carb cauliflower. Prepare a sauce to season crispy cauliflower florets.

Ingredients:

- Cauliflower florets   4 cups
- Water   ½ cup
- Almond milk   ½ cup
- All-purpose flour   1 cup
- Garlic powder   2 teaspoons
- Cumin   1 teaspoon
- Paprika   1 teaspoon
- Black pepper   ¼ teaspoons
- Red hot sauce, kidney-friendly, low-sodium   1 cup
- Butter   1 tablespoon

Instructions:

1. Layer a baking sheet with parchment paper and grease it with oil.
2. Set oven to 400 degrees F (204 °C) and let preheat.
3. Add all ingredients except for butter and red hot sauce in a bowl and mix well.
4. Dip the cauliflower florets in the mixture and place them on the baking sheet.
5. Bake the cauliflower for 20 minutes in the oven until golden brown, flipping them halfway through.
6. Meanwhile, mix butter and hot sauce in a saucepan and place it over medium heat.
7. Stir and cook the sauce for 1 minute until butter is melted.
8. When the cauliflower is done, transfer the florets into a large bowl.
9. Pour in hot sauce and then toss well until the florets are evenly coated.
10. Spread the florets on the baking sheet.
11. Bake the florets for 15 minutes again.
12. Serve.

Turkey Burgers

Sodium – 136.8mg; **Potassium** - 399mg; **Phosphorus** - 279.5mg

Check with a kidney doctor or dietitian for guidelines to adjust protein intake.

Prep Time:	10 m	**Calories:**	254
Cook Time:	10 m	**Fat (g):**	13.8
Total Time:	20 m	**Protein (g):**	25.2
Servings:	4	**Carbs (g):**	7

Ingredients:

• Ground turkey	1 lb (454g)
• Zucchini, grated *corgetts*	1 cup
• Egg, large	1
• Panko bread crumbs	¼ cup
• Red onion, grated	¼ cup
• Garlic clove, minced	1
• Salt-free seasoning	1 teaspoon
• Black pepper	½ teaspoon
• Olive oil	1 tablespoon

Instructions:

1. Mix all the turkey burger ingredients in a bowl.
2. Make ½ inch thick patties out of this mixture.
3. Place a greased skillet on medium-high heat.
4. Cook the turkey burgers in the skillet for 5 minutes per side.
5. Serve warm.

Baked Asparagus

Sodium – 2.5mg; **Potassium** - 233.3mg; **Phosphorus** - 59.4mg

Prep Time:	10 m	Calories:	83.2
Cook Time:	10 m	Fat (g):	6.9
Total Time:	20 m	Protein (g):	2.5
Servings:	4	Carbs (g):	5

Ingredients:

- Asparagus   1 lb (454g)
- Olive oil   2 tablespoons
- Black pepper   ¼ teaspoon
- Lemon juice   1 tablespoon

Instructions:

1. Set oven to 400 degrees F (204 °C) and let preheat.
2. Cut the ends of the asparagus spears and peel the skins of the base of the asparagus.
3. Toss asparagus with olive oil and black pepper.
4. Place the asparagus on a baking sheet.
5. Bake for 10 minutes in the preheated oven.
6. When done, sprinkle with lemon juice and serve.

Dutch Apple Pancake

Sodium – 173.5mg; **Potassium** - 185.5mg; **Phosphorus** - 138.5mg

Prep Time:	15 m	**Calories:**	525.7
Cook Time:	25 m	**Fat (g):**	22.8
Total Time:	40 m	**Protein (g):**	8.4
Servings:	4	**Carbs (g):**	73.7

Have you tried the sweet and irresistible Dutch apple pancake before? Then comes a chance to try baking at home with basic ingredients.

Ingredients:

• Eggs	4
• All-purpose flour	½ cup
• Baking powder	½ teaspoon
• Almond milk	1 cup
• Vanilla extract	1 teaspoon
• Unsalted butter, melted	2 tablespoons
• Ground nutmeg	1 teaspoon
• Unsalted butter	¼ cup
• White sugar	½ cup + 1 tablespoon
• Ground cinnamon	½ teaspoon
• Tart apple, peeled, cored, and sliced	1 large

Instructions:

1. Beat eggs with 1 tablespoon of sugar in a large bowl.
2. Stir in baking powder, flour, and almond milk with constant mixing.
3. Add ½ teaspoon of nutmeg, melted butter, and vanilla, then mix until smooth.
4. Set oven to 425 degrees F (218 °C) and let preheat.
5. Add butter to a 10-inch skillet and melt it over medium heat.
6. Mix ½ teaspoon of nutmeg, cinnamon, and ¼ cup of sugar in a small bowl. Sprinkle this mixture over the butter.
7. Spread the apple slices in a skillet and drizzle the remaining sugar over the slices.
8. Place this pan over medium-high heat and cook until the mixture bubbles.
9. Pour the prepared batter on top of the apples.
10. Bake the pancake for 15 minutes in the oven, then reduce heat to 375 F (191 °C).
11. Bake this pancake again for 10 minutes.
12. Slice the pancake into wedges and serve.

Cranberry Bread

Sodium – 182.5mg; **Potassium** - 89mg; **Phosphorus** - 60.3mg

Prep Time:	10 m	**Calories:**	241.8
Cook Time:	1 h	**Fat (g):**	8.8
Total Time:	1 h 10 m	**Protein (g):**	4.7
Servings:	10	**Carbs (g):**	38.6

Here comes a loaded bread to serve in the breakfast or with any of your favorite meals!
The cranberry bread is a sweet and savory delight to enjoy.

Ingredients:

• All-purpose flour	2 cups (8.81 oz/250g)
• Baking soda	1 teaspoon
• Egg	1 large
• Brown sugar	½ cup (3.7 oz/105g)
• Granulated sugar	½ cup (3.52 oz/100g)
• Buttermilk	1 cup (8 fl. oz/240ml)
• Olive oil	1/3 cup (2.66 fl. oz/ 80ml)
• Vanilla extract	1 teaspoon
• Orange zest	2 teaspoons
• Cranberries, fresh	1 cup (3.88 oz/110g)

Instructions:

1. Switch on the oven, then set it to 350 degrees F (177°C) and let it preheat.
2. Meanwhile, take a 9-by-5 inches bread pan, grease it with oil and set it aside until required.
3. Mix baking soda and flour in a large bowl.
4. Beat egg with granulated sugar and brown sugar in another bowl.
5. Add orange zest, vanilla, oil, and buttermilk.
6. Mix well, then fold in the flour mixture, then mix until smooth.
7. Fold in cranberries, then mix evenly.
8. Spoon the dough into the prepared pan and then bake for 1 hour or more until the crust turned golden brown and passes the toothpick test; a toothpick should come out clean from the bread or else continue baking for another 10 minutes.
9. When done, let the bread cool in its pan for 10 minutes, then carefully lift out the bread and transfer it to a wire rack for 30 minutes or more until cooled.
10. Cut the bread into ten slices and then serve.

Linguine Shrimp Scampi With Garlic

Sodium – 93.3mg; **Potassium** - 131.6mg; **Phosphorus** - 190.6mg

Check with a kidney doctor or dietitian for guidelines to adjust protein intake.

Prep Time:	15 m	Calories:	369.1
Cook Time:	10 m	Fat (g):	13.2
Total Time:	25 m	Protein (g):	17.6
Servings:	6	Carbs (g):	43.8

Ingredients:

- Linguine   3/4 lb (340g)
- Unsalted butter   3 tablespoons
- Olive oil   2 ½ tablespoons
- Minced garlic   1 ½ tablespoons
- Large shrimp, peeled and deveined, without salt   1 lb (454g)
- Ground black pepper   ¼ teaspoon
- Parsley, chopped   1/3 cup
- Lemon zest grated   ½ lemon
- Lemon juice   ¼ cup
- Lemon, sliced in half-rounds   ¼
- Hot red pepper flakes   1/8 teaspoon

Instructions:

1. Cook linguine according to the package instructions without using salt.
2. Heat butter and olive oil in a large pot over medium heat.
3. Sauté garlic for 1 minute.
4. Stir in shrimp, black pepper, and cook for 5 minutes with occasional stirring.
5. Remove from the heat, then stir in red pepper flakes, lemon slices, lemon juice, lemon zest, and parsley.
6. Mix well, then add in linguine.
7. Toss well and serve.

Sweet Cherry Cobbler

Sodium – 75mg; **Potassium** - 199.5mg; **Phosphorus** - 53.4mg

Prep Time:	10 m	**Calories:**	300.1
Cook Time:	22 m	**Fat (g):**	3.4
Total Time:	32 m	**Protein (g):**	2.5
Servings:	8	**Carbs (g):**	67.3

Every sweet tooth will definitely love this quick and simple to make cherry cobbler. Serve this cobbler on all the special dinners.

Ingredients:

Cherry filling

- Sweet red cherries   5 cups
- Granulated sugar   2/3 cup
- Cornstarch   2 tablespoons
- Lemon juice   2 tablespoons
- Vanilla extract   1 teaspoon
- Almond extract   ¼ teaspoon

Cobbler topping

- All-purpose flour   1 cup
- Sugar   ½ cup
- Baking powder   1 teaspoon
- Ground cinnamon   ¼ teaspoon
- Unsalted butter, cubed   2 tablespoons
- Almond milk, cold   ½ cup

Instructions:

1. Set oven to 450 degrees F (232 °C) and let preheat.
2. Slice the cherries in half and remove their pits.
3. Add cherries, cornstarch, and sugar to a large saucepan.
4. Set the pan over medium heat and add lemon juice, almond extract, and vanilla extract.
5. Bring to a boil and cook for 7 minutes until the berries are soft.
6. Spread the cherry filling in an 8 inches baking pan.
7. For the topping, mix flour with cinnamon, butter, sugar, and baking powder in a bowl.
8. Pour in milk and mix until it makes a crumbly dough.
9. Spread the dough on top of the berry filling and bake for 15 minutes.
10. Slice and serve.

Peach Cobbler

Sodium – 204.2mg; **Potassium** - 190.5mg; **Phosphorus** - 73.4mg

Prep Time:	10 m	**Calories:**	438.8
Cook Time:	45 m	**Fat (g):**	12.1
Total Time:	55 m	**Protein (g):**	2.5
Servings:	8	**Carbs (g):**	83.1

Peach cobbler is a must for every dessert menu- So why not try this simple recipe and yet full of nutrients.

Ingredients:

• Unsalted butter	½ cup
• All-purpose flour	1 cup
• Sugar	2 cups
• Baking powder	1 tablespoon
• Almond milk	1 cup
• Fresh peach slices	4 cups
• Lemon juice	1 tablespoon
• Ground cinnamon	Optional

Instructions:

1. Set oven to 375 degrees F (190 °C) and let preheat.
2. Grease a 13x9 inches baking dish with melted butter.
3. Mix almond milk, 1 cup of sugar, baking powder, and flour in a bowl until smooth.
4. Pour the prepared batter into the baking dish.
5. Add peach slices, lemon juice, and 1 cup of sugar in a saucepan.
6. Bring to a boil over high heat with occasional stirring.
7. Spread the peaches over the batter and drizzle cinnamon on top.
8. Bake the peach cobbler for 45 minutes until golden brown.
9. Serve.

Blueberries, Cranberries, Strawberries Smoothie

Sodium – 1mg; **Potassium** - 117.6mg; **Phosphorus** - 18.4mg

Prep Time:	5 m	**Calories:**	39.3
Cook Time:	0 m	**Fat (g):**	0.3
Total Time:	5 m	**Protein (g):**	0.7
Servings:	3	**Carbs (g):**	9.8

Smoothies are always a delight for every serving table- now, you can make a creamy smoothie with this recipe.

Ingredients:

- Strawberries   1 cup
- Blueberries   ½ cup
- Cranberries   ½ cup
- Water   1 cup

Instructions:

1. Add all ingredients to a blender.
2. Press the pulse button and blend until smooth.
3. Serve.

Blueberry Pie

Sodium – 187.7mg; **Potassium** - 155.8mg; **Phosphorus** - 59.3mg

Prep Time:	10 m	**Calories:**	336.1
Cook Time:	1 h 5 m	**Fat (g):**	12.2
Total Time:	1 h 15 m	**Protein (g):**	4.4
Servings:	8	**Carbs (g):**	54.7

A blueberry pie is one special dessert recipe that everyone loves to have. Use this quick to bake recipe and enjoy.

Ingredients:

- Pie crust   2
- Fresh blueberries, rinsed   6 cups
- Lemon zest   1 teaspoon
- Lemon juice   1 tablespoon
- Cornstarch   ¼ cup
- Sugar   ½ cup
- Cinnamon   ½ teaspoon
- Egg   1
- Milk   1 tablespoon

Instructions:

1. Set oven to 425 degrees F (218 °C) and let preheat.
2. Prepare the filling and mix blueberries with cinnamon, lemon juice, lemon zest, cornstarch, and sugar in a saucepan.
3. Cook the berries until soft and mix well.
4. Allow the filling to cool and keep it aside.
5. Roll the pie crusts into 9-inch rounds.
6. Place the pie crust in a 9-inch pie pan and top it with berry filling.
7. Set the other pie crust on top.
8. Beat egg with milk and brush it over the pie.
9. Bake the pie for 20 minutes in the oven at 425 F (218 °C).
10. Reduce the heat to 350 F (177 °C) and bake for 40 minutes.
11. Allow the pie to cool and slice.

Lemon Curd

Sodium – 27mg; **Potassium** - 47.9mg; **Phosphorus** - 44.9mg

Prep Time:	5 m	**Calories:**	297.6
Cook Time:	10 m	**Fat (g):**	17.2
Total Time:	15 m	**Protein (g):**	2.5
Servings:	12	**Carbs (g):**	35

Do you want to have citrus rich curd to serve at the morning table? Well, here is the recipe that you should try.

Ingredients:

• Lemon juice	2/3 cup
• Granulated sugar	2 cups
• Zest from lemons	4 lemons
• Unsalted butter	1 cup
• Eggs, well beaten	4
• Egg yolk	1

Instructions:

1. Mix sugar with lemon zest and lemon juice in a suitable saucepan.
2. Warm this mixture, then add butter to melt and remove it from the heat.
3. Allow this mixture to cool, stir in eggs, egg yolk, beat well, and place it in a double boiler.
4. Mix and cook this mixture until it thickens.
5. Remove this curd from the boiler and mix well for 5 minutes.
6. Pass this curd through a strainer and store it in a mason jar.
7. Serve.

Raspberry Mint Limeade

Sodium – 24.5mg; **Potassium** - 78.1mg; **Phosphorus** - 11.6mg

Prep Time:	5 m	**Calories:**	53.8
Cook Time:	10 m	**Fat (g):**	0.2
Total Time:	15 m	**Protein (g):**	0.4
Servings:	6	**Carbs (g):**	14.3

Beat the heat, and try this raspberry mint limeade to give yourself a refreshing boost. This recipe has a balanced blend of berries with lime and mint to create a great flavor.

Ingredients:

- Frozen raspberries   1 cup
- Water   1 ½ cups
- Sugar   ¼ cup
- Mint   8 sprigs
- Lime juice   1 cup
- Soda water   3 cups
- Ice cubes

Instructions:

1. Mix sugar, water, and raspberries in a suitable saucepan.
2. Cook this berry mixture on medium heat for 5 minutes until berries are soft.
3. Add mint sprigs and then remove the pan from the heat.
4. Allow the mixture to cool at room temperature, then remove the mint.
5. Puree the berry mixture with a hand blender.
6. Strain the mixture through and discard the solids.
7. Mix the berry juice with lime juice and then divide it into 6 serving glasses.
8. Pour soda water into each glass, add ice cubes, and garnish with lime wedges and raspberries.
9. Serve.

Strawberry Blueberry Overnight Oats

Sodium – 83mg; **Potassium** - 471mg; **Phosphorus** - 161.3mg

Prep Time:	5 m	Calories:	325
Cook Time:	0 m	Fat (g):	2.7
Total Time:	5 m	Protein (g):	6
Servings:	2	Carbs (g):	74

This is an effortless oatmeal recipe that you would not want to miss out on this menu.
Use your favorite combination of berries to bring variation.

Ingredients:

- Rolled oats (1 serving per week)   1 cup
- Almond milk   1 cup
- Strawberries   1 cup
- Ground cinnamon   ¼ teaspoon
- Maple syrup   ¼ cup
- Blueberries   ½ cup

Instructions:

1. Destem the strawberries and slice them into quarters.
2. Add layers of oats, almond milk, blueberries, cinnamon, strawberries, and maple syrup in two mason jars.
3. Cover the lids and refrigerate them for 5 hours.
4. Serve.

Blueberry Smoothie

Sodium – 152mg; **Potassium** - 212 mg; **Phosphorus** - 4.8mg

Prep Time:	1 m	Calories:	103
Cook Time:	1 m	Fat (g):	2.5
Total Time:	2 m	Protein (g):	1.3
Servings:	1	Carbs (g):	19.1

This glass of Blueberry smoothie in the morning or in between meals is one good way to revitalize yourself.

Ingredients:

• Frozen blueberries	¼ cup
• Almond milk	1 cup
• Honey	1 teaspoon
• Fresh mint	1 sprig
• Ice cubes	

Instructions:

1. Blend blueberries with almond milk, honey, mint, and ice in a food processor for 1 minute.
2. Serve.

Cranberry Oatmeal Cookies

Sodium – 14.5mg; **Potassium** - 110.6mg; **Phosphorus** - 84mg

Prep Time:	15 m	**Calories:**	220.5
Cook Time:	15 m	**Fat (g):**	8.8
Total Time:	30 m	**Protein (g):**	6
Servings:	12	**Carbs (g):**	31.9

These cookies are no ordinary ones- they have a unique texture and an irresistible flavor to enjoy during your snack breaks.

Ingredients:

• Unsalted butter	½ cup
• Granulated sugar	½ cup
• Egg, large	1
• All-purpose flour	¼ cup
• Vanilla extract	1 teaspoon
• Cinnamon	½ teaspoon
• Vanilla whey protein powder	1 ½ oz. (42.5g)
• Applesauce	1 cup
• Rolled oats	3 cups
• Dried cranberries	½ cup

Instructions:

1. Preheat oven to 350 F (177 °C).
2. Layer a baking sheet with parchment paper.
3. Beat butter with sugar in a bowl with an electric mixer.
4. Stir in cinnamon, vanilla extract, protein powder, flour, and egg, then mix well.
5. Add applesauce, then mix well.
6. Fold in cranberries and oats, then mix evenly.
7. Scoop the dough with ¼ cup scoop onto a baking sheet.
8. Flatten the cookies and bake for 15 minutes until golden brown.
9. Allow the cookies to cool and serve.

Raspberry Pear Sorbet

Sodium – 1mg; **Potassium** - 114.8mg; **Phosphorus** - 20mg

Prep Time:	10 m	Calories:	107.6
Cook Time:	12 h 10 m	Fat (g):	0.4
Total Time:	12 h 20 m	Protein (g):	0.8
Servings:	6	Carbs (g):	27.5

Sorbets are another good way to enjoy your favorite fruits, and this pear and raspberries sorbet can be your way to enjoy some!

Ingredients:

- Sugar — ½ cup
- Water — 1 cup
- Fresh raspberries — 12 oz (340g)
- Large pear halves, canned in juice — 2
- Lime juice — 1/3 cup
- Pear liqueur — 1 tablespoon
- Fresh raspberries — To serve

Instructions:

1. Mix sugar and 1 cup of water in a suitable saucepan and cook for 3 minutes on a simmer, then allow it to cool.
2. Puree 12 oz raspberries, pear liqueur, lime juice, and pear in a blender until smooth.
3. Stir in sugar syrup and mix well.
4. Spread this mixture in an 8x8 inch baking pan, then cover and freeze for 4 hours.
5. Blend the ice cream mixture in the food processor for 30 seconds.
6. Transfer the mixture to a container, then cover to freeze for 8 hours.
7. Garnish with raspberries and serve.

Italian Lemonade

Sodium – 2.3mg; **Potassium** - 97.3mg; **Phosphorus** - 11.3mg

Prep Time:	5 m	**Calories:**	278
Cook Time:	7 m	**Fat (g):**	0.08
Total Time:	12 m	**Protein (g):**	0.35
Servings:	6	**Carbs (g):**	73.5

Fresh basil lemonade is one of the refreshing drink to beat the heat. This lemonade has a very balanced blend of sugar, water, basil, and lemon juice.

Ingredients:

- Fresh basil, washed and stemmed   1 bunch
- Sugar   2 cups
- Water   1 cup
- Lemon juice   2 cups
- Coldwater   2 cups

Instructions:

1. Mix 1 cup of water, 2 cups of sugar, and basil in a saucepan, then cook for 5 minutes.
2. Strain this mixture and allow it to cool.
3. Blend lemon juice with 2 cups of cold water and basil syrup in a blender for 30 seconds.
4. Serve.

Strawberries and Pineapple Smoothie

Sodium – 78.5mg; **Potassium** - 490mg; **Phosphorus** - 47.7mg

Prep Time:	5 m	**Calories:**	158.5
Cook Time:	0 m	**Fat (g):**	2
Total Time:	5 m	**Protein (g):**	2.5
Servings:	2	**Carbs (g):**	36.6

Smooth and creamy strawberry pineapple smoothies are everyone's favorite. Try this recipe to serve in breakfast or at snack time.

Ingredients:

- Vanilla almond milk   1 cup
- Strawberries   2 cups No
- Fresh pineapple chunks   2 cups

Instructions:

1. Add almond milk, pineapple, and strawberries to a blender.
2. Press the pulse button and blend until smooth.
3. Serve.

Fruit Salad

Sodium – 4.5mg; **Potassium** - 380.2mg; **Phosphorus** - 63mg

Prep Time:	5 m	Calories:	197.5
Cook Time:	0 m	Fat (g):	1.2
Total Time:	5 m	Protein (g):	2.5
Servings:	4	Carbs (g):	48.9

A refreshing bowl of fruit salad is all you need to make your day better.

Ingredients:

- Fresh strawberries, halved ~~X~~ *No.*   1 lb (454g)
- Fresh blueberries   12 oz (340g)
- Fresh raspberries   12 oz (340g)

Honey lime dressing

- Honey   ¼ cup
- Lime zest   2 teaspoons

Instructions:

1. Toss blueberries, raspberries, and strawberries in a salad bowl.
2. Mix lime zest and honey in a small bowl.
3. Pour this mixture over the fruits and toss well to coat.
4. Serve.

Printed in Great Britain
by Amazon